HEROIC BROTHERS
OF THE CIVIL WAR

by
Bill Cushing

HEROIC BROTHERS
OF THE CIVIL WAR

by Bill Cushing

Southern Arizona Press
Sierra Vista, Arizona

Heroic Brothers of the Civil War

By Bill Cushing

First Edition

Author: Bill Cushing
Editor: Paul Gilliland
Formatting: Southern Arizona Press
Cover Design: Bill Cushing
All Artwork: Public Domain unless otherwise indicated

Published by Southern Arizona Press
Sierra Vista, Arizona 85635
www.SouthernArizonaPress.com

ISBN: 978-1-960038-47-0

Historical Non-Fiction, Military History, U.S. Civil War, Educational

Dedicated in gratitude to all those who have given.

Foreword

Heroic Brothers of the Civil War is an intriguing account of the heroic feats of the Cushing brothers—Lon and Will—during pivotal campaigns of the War Between the States. Bill Cushing artfully describes the actions of his ancestors, their motivations, their leadership, and most interestingly, their vast differences.

One a serious, methodical, and calculating Army officer and the other a brash, bold, almost reckless Navy officer, the Cushing brothers shared a sense of duty and a leadership compass that produced courageous yet compassionate action in preparation for and in the execution of battle.

This book tells the story of tough but caring leadership, battlefield valor, leadership by example, physical courage, and the bonds between American warriors that are timeless and were found in the battles that the Cushings fought and are prominent characteristics of today's U.S. Armed Forces.

— Major General Walt Lord (U. S. Army, ret.)

Contents

West Point Cadet Alonzo H. Cushing, Senior Picture

THE LAST MAN

Alonzo Cushing was not sure what had awakened him so early this Friday, July 3rd, 1863.

Perhaps it was the creeping heat of a summer day in Gettysburg, Pennsylvania—him being used to the cooler climate of upstate New York. Perhaps his restlessness was from the anxious feeling pervading the air like smoke from the weapons fired over the past two days of intense and continuous fighting. Whatever the cause, the young Army officer rose and dressed to prepare for whatever might come from the Confederacy's Army of Northern Virginia.

As a cadet at West Point, Alonzo, or Lon as he preferred, was in the top half of the class of 1861 and part of a corps that graduated ahead of schedule when the Civil War became inevitable. Many of the cadets from the Southern states had resigned West Point to filter back to their home states. Like his younger brother Will, Lon was a prolific letter-writer, and in a letter to his mother, he expressed regret that none of the Southern cadets leaving the academy in anticipation of war were ranked ahead of him. That meant those departures did not help his class standing. He began his military career attached to Battery A of the 4th U. S. Artillery Regiment.

First established in 1821, Battery A was composed mainly of Irish and German veterans. He had only been an officer for a month when the unit fought in the First Battle of Bull Run—the first major engagement of the Civil War and a disaster for the Union.

Lon not only met expectations, he exceeded them. His superiors trusted his judgment and transferred him to the Army of the Potomac as a topographical engineer. This assignment made him responsible for surveying potential battlegrounds to aid in strategy; it also put him in the Army's elite. Engineers were considered the intellectual component and usually moved up the ranks rapidly.

11

Still, he yearned more for action and saw artillery as his steppingstone, but those initial duties surveying and drawing maps did prove advantageous after he returned to take command of his original unit. When Lon was reassigned and in charge of Battery A, one of the first to welcome him back was Frederick Füger, now his First Sergeant.

"Willkommen, junger welpe!" shouted the boisterous older man, wrapping his arms around Lon as a father might greet a long-lost son. "And look at him. Shaving now."

First Sergeant and Medal of Honor recipient Frederick Füger

Then, recalling the situation, he composed himself to step back, back stiffened, as he shouted, "Attention!" Still, Lon had been flattered by the moment, especially since his own father had died 16 years earlier when Lon was only six. His boyish face struggled to suppress a happy grin. He was sure more than ever that Battery A was where he was meant to be.

Now 22, Lon was already a veteran of four of the major Civil War battles. At Fredericksburg, he had been given a battlefield promotion to Captain and then brevetted as a Major during Chancellorsville. For an incoming officer, these temporary battlefield promotions were unusual, and other than classmate George Custer, no other Civil War officer in the Army had been promoted so quickly and at such a young age.

Now fully dressed, Lon left his tent to go to the mess area. He filled his kit with a typical battlefield breakfast of hard tack and salt pork to be washed down with some strong black coffee.

"You mind?" he asked Captain William Arnold, a fellow artillery commander from Rhode Island. Lon pointed his coffee cup to an empty chair near Arnold.

"Please," the older officer said. The two fought together at Fredericksburg but had gotten to know each other at Chancellorsville, fighting side-by-side during that battle. President Lincoln publicly noted Lon's "conspicuous gallantry at the battle" of Chancellorsville. While the latter campaign also proved disastrous for the Union, the two officers acquitted themselves well and formed a bond beyond respect.

"Do you ever find it strange to read about a battle you'd fought in?" Lon asked as he sat. "It's as if newspapers knew more about the action than we. I only recall seeing little more than smoke and hearing only noise." Taking a sip of coffee, Lon exhaled before he continued. "Everything looks frantic and confused while some 'expert' seems to have it all figured out."

"Remember," Arnold answered. "Those reporters are usually on the high ground and talking with the generals. We're stuck in the middle of the battle."

Like Lon, Arnold's Yankee bloodline stretched back to the Revolutionary War. Both families shared a Puritan heritage, a faith that abhorred the notion of slavery. Those values had been instilled by Lon's mother, now a widow for a decade and a half. He hoped to write her once the day's fighting was over.

Second Lieutenant Cushing: Battery A, 4th Artillery

Lon turned his attention back to the day at hand.

"Have you gotten your orders yet?" Arnold asked as Lon finished up his meal.

"Not yet," Lon said, wiping some crumbs from his lower lip. "You?"

"Actually," the other officer said. "I can tell you yours as well. I am to take a position to your right. Both of us will entrench before the 71st Infantry from Pennsylvania."

"Before? You mean the infantry won't be our front line?"

"Not today," Arnold answered. "There's no real slope for them to create a front, so they will take their position behind our guns."

Lon did not care for the idea that his own troops would not have the added protection of some perimeter riflemen.

"Do you know that Lee and I share the same birthday?" he asked, hoping to lighten his mood after recalling how Fredericksburg lasted four days compared to the past two days of fighting in the meadows and plains of this small Pennsylvania town. More men had already been killed in action here than were lost the entire time at Fredericksburg.

"Well," Arnold answered, "he's still alive and kicking, so here's to you living as long as he has."

Lon took a final look across the Pennsylvania fields separating the two armies and stood to fill his canteen with water before making his way to officially receive his orders.

"Wonder what 'Granny Lee' is thinking today?" Arnold asked, using the nickname that many had attached to the commander of the Army of Northern Virginia because of his extreme caution as a military leader.

Lon smiled at the joke and gave Arnold an informal salute as he left to prepare, but both knew what was on Lee's mind today. Most Union soldiers understood Lee had to secure a victory if the Confederacy had any chance of getting help from Europe. A decisive triumph against the Union in northern territory would go a long way in doing that. After all, the South's general reasoned, the French had supported the colonists less than a century before.

After Lon received his own orders and conferred on supplies and positioning, he returned to his tent to prepare mentally for the task ahead. Sitting outside the open tent flaps, he lit his pipe and thought on his younger brother William. Lon wondered how Will was faring.

Born less than 22 months apart, the two grew up inseparable and devoted to each other, yet they lived their lives in vastly different ways, each distinct in his own personality. Lon was contemplative while Will lived so impulsively as to be almost impetuous. The older was ambitious and meticulous; the younger audacious, mercurial. As an officer, Lon exhibited the deliberation of a chess master, always staying aware of possible consequences. Lon rooted his decisions in probabilities and reality; Will never envisioned any outcome other than success.

Will was not a stellar student but had been dismissed from Annapolis for disciplinary, not academic problems. Never the best behaved, he had exceeded the allowable number of demerits after openly humiliating one of his professors. Lon had feared his younger brother would get into trouble but not so close to graduation. Reinstated by the Navy after the war broke out, Will was assigned on ships blockading supplies to the South. Such duty was tedious and trying, and Lon doubted his brother's demeanor could tolerate the demands of that particular task.

For Lon's part, lack of action was rarely part of the itinerary, nor would it be on this day—this July 3rd. He was assigned 126 men and six cannons with the task of defending Cemetery Ridge, a low rise at the northern end of the Union forces

Lon summoned First Sergeant Füger and had him call the men to their stations. He went ahead to survey his situation and equipment

From the other side of the battlefield, Brigadier General Lewis Armistead, one of Lee's most respected and intelligent officers, received his own orders, which included taking the area Lon's troops had been assigned. Lee was comforted by the sheer size of his numbers. With nearly 12,000 men under Armistead's command, Lee was convinced that the Virginians could overwhelm the much smaller contingent of Yankees. Besides the 1,000 to one numerical advantage of his regiment, Armistead was assured that the intense bombardment from over 150 Southern cannons would demoralize the Union troops if not demolish their artillery, itself limited to about 80 pieces, many already damaged and practically useless.

At around 8 a.m., Lon heard that battery begin.

Confederate artillery lobbed a barrage of shells across the field at the Union defensive positions, creating a thunderous noise that shook roof tiles of buildings loose while people as far away as a mile thought a storm was coming. In many ways, it was a maelstrom as Gettysburg's last day marked "the great artillery duel" of the Civil War.

Lon's battery stood at "The Angle," a spot so named because of the stone walls that met at an intersection that formed the troops into the shape of a fishhook. Surrounded by a thicket of trees, the Angle overlooked a vast plain. Having already tried to penetrate the center of the Yankee lines on July 1st and the southern portion the next day, it became the focal point where General Lee ordered "Pickett's Charge" to take place on the third and final day of the conflict.

But before that charge could even happen, the morning's shelling had done its job, hitting three chests of Lon's ammunition, killing several men far too soon, and damaging several of his cannons. The explosions forced Lon to withhold fire so that he could safeguard his remaining ammunition as well as relocate the three moveable cannons he had left.

At noon, rations were delivered to the Union soldiers as the violent action came to a stop to allow both sides' weapons to cool. Besides eating, it allowed the two armies to assess the damage so far, make adjustments, and allow the weapons to cool down.

Before the cannonade could continue, Lon moved his guns forward to take a spot behind a low stone wall, preparing for the Confederate infantry's inevitable attack. Once Pickett began his charge, among the heaviest hit were the positions near Lon.

Lon had three guns but only enough men to operate two of them. Infantrymen, most of them attached to the Pennsylvania 71st, were called to replace wounded artillerymen, the replacements themselves soon became casualties.

Lieutenant Cushing on the Gettysburg battlefield (center, right of flag)

One Pennsylvanian was so badly wounded, he pleaded for someone, anyone to put him out of his misery. When no one would, he pulled out his pistol and ended his own life. The battle intensified as a hailstorm of bullets mixed with the whistle or shriek of cannon fire.

"Hold your positions," Lon screamed to the collapsing line of men. "First man to leave his post, I'll blow his brains out!"

His refusal to retreat kept the shaken and confused troops in place. He was now down to two guns, but who dared leave when this almost angelic-looking officer stood his ground?

Around 1:40 in the afternoon, a cannon ball exploded near Lon, its fragments tearing open both his thighs, ripping cloth and flesh and his genitals as it went by, becoming his first wound. He stayed his post.

A little before 2:30, the Confederate infantry began its slow march toward Lon's position in a line stretching almost a mile across, presenting a show of strength so massive that one Union officer later described it as "magnificent, grim, and irresistible."

If such was the case, then Lon and his troops became the object to the South's "irresistible force."

Captain Arnold's unit had suffered the least damage, so he redirected his line of fire toward Lon's section of the Angle in the hope of helping his comrade-in-arms in defending against Armistead's advance.

Lon was then wounded in his shoulder. He refused to remove himself from the line for a doctor to examine him. Lon viewed this as a practical matter more than heroics. Amputation had become the preferred treatment of frontline surgeons. Lon preferred to deal with Confederate rifles rather than a bone-cutting saw. Now wounded twice, he stayed on, perhaps resigned to the fact of his death. He became a soldier seeking his particular bullet.

"Here comes the Johnnies," one infantryman shouted out as Armistead's troops let loose the blood-chilling "Rebel yell" the Southerners made famous.

Defending his position during the charge, Lon refused to leave his post despite the bleeding and pain of his injuries. He saw that there was no way his force of less than 40 or 50 men could hold up against the thousands of butternut-clad troops moving toward his position.

"If I might, sir," First Sergeant Füger growled in his thick German accent, "perhaps you'd best to be getting back to the medical station."

Lon refused. Instead, he ordered his First Sergeant to prepare a triple-cannister load for a final shot.

"Cushing," commanded a superior officer, "go to the rear!"

"No, Sir," he shouted back, "I stay right here and fight it out or die in the attempt."

Bleeding out from his earlier wounds, Lon realized this was his last day on earth. He stopped intestines from spilling out by clamping the flat side of a stray food canteen against his stomach. Leaning against his remaining cannon, Lon sucked at a fleshless thumb. He had not been wearing the padded lather glove that protected handlers from the searing heat of venting gases that escaped after each volley, so that finger had been burned to the bone.

With the enemy within a hundred yards and almost on the ground where the last gun had been drawn up, Lon stood as straight as he was able.

"Give them one more shot." he cried, adding above the din, "Goodbye!"

Lieutenant Cushing's last shot

Then, an iron ball from a charging infantryman's musket struck him in the mouth, traveling through his throat and out the back of his head. He stumbled and fell into First Sergeant. Füger's arms, killed instantly. The cannon shot represented the last of Battery A's ammunition and was fired by the steadfast First Sergeant Füger.

It was only one cannon shot, but it tore a wide hole in the advancing enemy, now inside the Angle and among the remains of Battery A. Confederate troops continued climbing the rise as Armistead's men hurdled the fence line and came through the smoke, but Lon and his men had delayed the attack long enough for reinforcements to arrive and beat back the charge, allowing the Union to win the battle and later the war itself.

On July 4th, the day after Lee and his Army of Northern Virginia retreated, it began to rain as if nature wished to wash the site clean of the blood soaking it from the bodies littered across the fields. Gettysburg, historically called the "high water mark of the

Confederacy," was perhaps best identified by one of its surviving combatants as "a bountiful harvest for the Angel of Death." That quote is hardly hyperbolic. Of the 175,000 involved in the fight, around 50,000 were either wounded, captured, or missing while over 7,000 were killed.

As to Lon, he died six months short of his 23rd birthday.

In the poem *John Brown's Body*, Stephen Vincent Benét called him "the last man at the last gun."

> *Cushing ran down the last of his guns to the battle-line.*
> *The rest had been smashed to scrap by Lee's artillery fire.*
> *He held his guts in his hand as the charge came up to the wall*
> *And his gun spoke out for him once before he fell to the ground.*

Excerpt from *John Brown's Body, Book Seven*
by Stephen Vincent Benét, 1928

From that time forward, the Battery A, 4th Artillery Regiment, would exist under the name of "Cushing's Battery" and now operates out of New York state as a ceremonial unit.

Monument to Lieutenant Alonzo H. Cushing
Gettysburg Battlefield
Photo courtesy of David Carra

Still, it was not until November of 2014—following decades of petitions and letters to Congress and the White House from family, military historians, and Civil War buffs—that Alonzo Hereford Cushing was at last awarded the Medal of Honor of the Civil War.

Lieutenant Alonzo H. Cushing's Medal of Honor and plaque at the Gettysburg National Battlefield Visitor Center.
Photo courtesy of Teresa Scott Hoggard.

Alonzo H. Cushing Grave Marker
West Point Cemetery

Lieutenant Commander William B. Cushing
Painting by Robert Hinckley, 1912

THE FIRST SEAL

Navy Lieutenant William Barker Cushing, "Will" informally, became the first in his family to learn of his brother Lon's death while fighting in the Battle of Gettysburg.

Will was at Naval Headquarters in Washington D.C. when couriers delivered word of the battle, its victorious outcome but also its losses. He was a deck officer for the USS Minnesota, a blockade ship cruising the mouth of the Roanoke River in North Carolina, when a messenger interrupted the briefings to deliver the news.

Two years earlier, in July of 1861, he affirmed his dedication to Lon by proclaiming, "If the Rebels should kill him I should become a fiend."

In many ways, that is exactly what he did—just not the way he planned

Upon hearing of the death, Will requested a transfer from the Navy to the Army, hoping for command of the 4th Artillery to honor the brother he loved so dearly. Fortunately for the Union and in many ways history, the Army did not cooperate since Will achieved unlikely feats of daring throughout his Naval career.

Two months after his brother's death, while standing mid-watch, he took the USS Minnesota's helm to chase down and collide with a Confederate blockade runner, but that only marked one incident among many.

In his youth, he was sturdy—almost burly, headstrong, and hasty, qualities he did not shed when entering the Naval Academy in 1857 at 14, an even earlier age than his brother. Now only 19 years old, he was the youngest lieutenant in the Navy, which might not have seemed possible given how his military life had started. His family used political connections to get him into Annapolis hoping to instill personal discipline in the young man.

Despite the Cushing involvement in the political realm of the United States, Will had no interest in such things. In fact, he generally disdained politics, once writing, "I went up to the new house of representatives and while there listened to enough nonsense to last me a year."

As a midshipman, however, his love for the Navy took a fierce hold over him. The youngest of four brothers, Will intended "to see every nook and corner of this little world that is to be seen." In his journals, he once proclaimed, "I had rather be an officer on board a man-of-war than the President of the United States."

Not being political in any real sense, he never looked at the big picture. As a student, Will was not very serious, especially if he saw no practical end to a course of study, and at the time, Annapolis focused primarily on a Classical education. He excelled in classes focusing on the tactical or military aspects of his chosen career such as gunnery, navigation, or seamanship classes. English, history, or physical science held no interest. He saw no purpose in them.

His behavior was equally comical and rebellious. Will was known for playing pranks on both staff and fellow classmates such as propping buckets of water over the tops of doors to douse unsuspecting entrants. At times, he fabricated a grappling hook and rope to snag jugs of tea steeping on mess hall windowsills meant for faculty, later lowering the emptied container back to its ledge.

Then there was his Moses imitation.

"Platoon leader Cushing," barked his company commander, "what in the name of all that is holy were you thinking?"

"About what, sir?" Will replied, a quizzical look plastered on his face.

"You marched your unit right into College Creek today."

"I was acting guidon bearer for the company, sir; we were in forward march."

The upper-class officer's frustration boiled over.

"And you know damned good and well that the roadway bends to the east toward the river there," he shouted, his face reddening and his nostrils flaring from anger.

"Of course, sir," Will said, deadpan. "But we never got the order to 'wheel right,' so I continued marching forward—as commanded."

"And you know that the officer commanding your unit stutters!" Slamming his fist against the desk, the ranting midshipman shook it in pain. Will's brigade commander, sitting to the side, worked to suppress a smile as the other continued his tirade. "He couldn't get the words out in time; it is your duty to accommodate such a situation when it arises."

"Sorry, sir," Will said, feigning ignorance. "I was simply following orders."

"Very well: now follow this. You just earned ten demerits."

"Thank you, sir," Will replied, standing, saluting in mocking precision, and leaving the room, again garnering points against him for actions born out of his attitude.

Will held the distinction of accumulating excessive demerits every year, changing his conduct only as the count began approaching a number that would lead to expulsion. The following year, he would go right back to his normal patterns of mischief.

While he might have gotten away with many of these acts, what did not help was a tendency to question authority figures for whom he had no respect, including faculty.

He was nearly expelled from the academy for dousing a Spanish instructor with a bucket of cold water as the man was on his way out to try and woo some women in town. After Will drew an insulting sketch of the same instructor, in a class he was not doing very well in anyway, the academy's superintendent—a very conservative traditionalist preferring the previous practice of culling officers from the "right" families—saw an opportunity. He coerced Will into signing his formal resignation from Annapolis on March 23, 1861.

The Civil War began less than two weeks later, which gave Will a chance for redemption. He traveled to Washington D.C. to plead the case for his reinstatement to a cousin who had a connection to Gideon Welles, the Secretary of the Navy.

After he returned to the fold, Will defined his career with incontestable bravery that was almost manic. Once aboard his first ship, he wrote to a cousin: "Where there is danger in battle, there will I be, for I will gain a name in this war." The war offered numerous chances for him to do so.

Existing warships of the Navy were designed for oceangoing battles, so they drew too much draft to enter most of the coastal rivers. The Union's strategy was to use its naval forces to blockade supplies and weapons coming to the Confederacy. Will found himself stationed at the mouth of the Cape Fear River in North Carolina since its twisting rivers and hidden inlets allowed Rebel blockade runners and foreign vessels relative success in running contraband through the region.

Finding action wherever and whenever he could, Will was credited with numerous captures. In May 1861, he had a hand in taking five schooners including the first prize of the war, a tobacco runner. By the time he was 19, he was given command of the USS Ellis, a gunboat. In one two-week period, he boarded and seized two merchant vessels, one holding cargo worth $75,000 and the next with an inventory valued at twice that—an impressive bounty that allowed him a certain leeway although his defiant nature did push limits.

By its nature, blockade duty was one that required patience, never Will's strength or even a minor attribute. Waiting was not in his character, so he often took things into his own hands. He would sneak off to counter the boredom of the squadron's assigned task, making daring and risky assaults on Hatteras region forts.

On numerous occasions, his superior officers wanted to "bring him before the mast" for punishment after each incident.

The problem was that every time he strayed, he managed to accomplish some task that no one else seemed capable of. By the time word of what he had done moved up the chain of command, his superiors were stymied from action by a newspaper article publicly touting the young officer's heroics. In one instance, the USS Ellis ran aground trying to return and had to be destroyed. An official Naval board of inquiry convened to investigate the loss of its ship. During the hearings, they learned that he had destroyed ten Confederate vessels along with an important processing plant. Faced with that information, even the admiral he served not only conceded his worth as a leader but wrote a letter commending "Lieutenant Cushing's coolness, courage, and conduct."

Will became an icon for personal bravery that bordered on bravado, and readers loved the daring young Naval officer depicted in the news. While he did not follow orders very well, he embodied the later military idea of adapt, improvise, and overcome.

And he is unquestionably remarkable in the naval history of the 19th century. Thus, he's acquired many labels as the first: the first commando, the original special ops sailor, the first "SEAL". It became obvious the young officer could not contend with the monotony of blockade duty, so the admiralty decided to let him loose, provided he inform them what he was planning.

That concession paid off handsomely as the young lieutenant produced two noteworthy successes within months of each other in 1864.

In February, Will proposed taking a contingent of men to kidnap Brigadier General Louis Hebert, the regional Confederate commander. Once he secured permission, he took to the task with gusto. He began the mission by approaching the town from a direction that would fool those on shore that his craft was moving downriver and most likely friendly.

Lieutenant William Barker Cushing

He got to the residence only to discover Hebert was not there. Still, he could not resist tweaking the general's nose a bit.

"My Dear General," Will wrote on a note card he left propped against a candlestick on the dining room table. "I deeply regret that you were not at home when I called. Very respectfully, W.B. Cushing."

Even the Confederates admired that kind of brass, and several of them made note of the Navy's renegade.

Admiral Samuel Lee, head of the squadron, decided to give Will free rein to form his own command and hunt blockade runners. In three months, Will got another chance to prove his cunning when the CSS Raleigh emerged from the river and attacked the Union fleet. Will immediately seized on a new idea: rather than defeating the CSS Raleigh, he would capture it.

On a moonlit evening, Will and 15 volunteers boarded a 30-foot cutter to find the ironclad warship. To get closer to the vessel, he took a veering and crooked path to deceive Rebel guards on shore that he was retreating. Then, some passing clouds blocked the moon. He took advantage of the natural cover for the more direct route upriver.

Upon arrival, the team discovered the Raleigh had run aground and split its keel. It was mired in the muck of the riverbank near Wilmington, North Carolina, making its capture moot. The trip appeared to have been wasted time. However, Will took the opportunity to observe and map the city's defenses, turning what might have disheartened others into an intelligence coup.

In addition, one of his crew captured a Confederate rider carrying mail. Going through the bag's contents, they found letters containing information about the size of a garrison in a nearby fort, an inventory of its supplies, and the deployment of its guns.

Even this was not enough to placate Will. Whether bravery, audacity, or a bit of both, he donned the courier's coat and hat and rode the horse to a general store. Using Confederate money from the mailbag, he bought food and supplies. This raid proved its worth in terms of information and material; its boldness convinced the young officer's superiors that they had access to a rare talent, a man who combined intelligence with cunning. As a result of his earlier adventures, they tagged him as the candidate to confront and hopefully neutralize another Confederate ironclad, the CSS Albemarle.

Engraving of the CSS Albermarle during the battle in the Roanoke River depicted by A. Stachie

Known to Union sailors as "the Confederates' Roanoke River bully," the CSS Albemarle had established itself as the unrivaled power of the river. After attacking and inflicting serious damage to four Union gunboats during one battle with only slight damage to itself, one senior commander of Union naval forces in the region conceded that "the ram has possession of the river." Its armor was so effectively constructed, that cannon balls actually shattered into pieces, sometimes causing added damage to the crews firing them as shrapnel from the rounds ricocheted. During another confrontation that lasted three hours against six Union battleships, all were damaged while the CSS Albermarle left both undamaged and without suffering a single casualty.

The Union Navy tried several raids to disable the craft, but direct attacks were made difficult by the Confederate fortifications dotting the shores leading to its dock. Attempts to use moored torpedoes like floating mines failed as well because its armor extended down its entire gunwale. In August of 1864, a lure was set out in hope of ambushing the ship, which resulted in the capture of ten of the men lying in wait.

After brainstorming several ideas—none of them feasible—the Navy realized it needed someone able to conceive a decisive and destructive response. The admiralty agreed that Will was the perfect person for the task even though they considered the feat impossible.

"Impossibilities are for the timid," Will countered after hearing the idea. Besides, for him it was personal. One of his closest friends was killed during one of the attacks by the seemingly invincible monster. When offered the mission, he promised, "I shall never rest until I have avenged his death."

Once the Navy offered him the challenge, little else needed to be done but to wait for him to hatch his plan. This certainly was Will's territory, for he took his time despite his personal animus after losing both his brother to the war and a close friend to that particular ship.

Now sitting in an office of the Naval Shipyard in Brooklyn, New York, he contemplated the project before him. Assessing the enemy vessel, Will scribbled notes about the CSS Albermarle:
"200' L
"50' W
"—extra wt/armor affects speed&maneuverability."
Early eyewitnesses reported that its deck held two 6.4-inch double-banded rifles along with a moveable cannon that could be shifted to fire from any of several different places. Then there was CSS Albermarle's apparent invulnerability. Sailors engaged in earlier battles with it recalled cannonballs bouncing off its thick iron hide, and, according to available intelligence, it was four inches thick in places and protected by nearly a foot and a half of wood backing.

Will hoped to board and "take her alive" but knew such a feat was unlikely given the number of guards he expected to be protecting such a valued weapon. Barring success with that idea, his next option was to approach the much larger vessel with what seemed a boat so small it would be deemed unworthy of much attention. From there, he and his men could explode a charge underneath the CSS Albermarle and, if not sink it, at least render it useless.

He paused, clenching the pencil between closed teeth, and thought. It was the ship's combination of fire power with its protective measures that became Will's priorities.

Will soon deduced that its weakness was, quite literally, the beast's underbelly. He would attack it from below the surface rather than butting heads with it directly in open waters. Success rested on getting close enough to inflict the damage.

"May work," Will muttered to himself "The trick is stealth."

Leaving his office, he went out to the yards and gathered some shipwrights, taking them to the wharf. He had already seen two boats he wanted to use. He chose them since they operated on low pressure steam engines, making them the quietest potential attack craft.

"That's the lead boat," he pointed to the larger of the pair. "I want it outfitted with a hinged stem that can be mounted with a moveable spar. Make sure there is a halyard to raise and lower the boom."

He then visited the gunnery sheds to acquire a torpedo, a fairly new weapon but one that a Confederate submarine had used successfully about eight months before; it seemed a good starting point. He approached the chief gunner and challenged him to design a method of mounting a torpedo at one end of the lever that could be lowered into the water ahead of the attack boat while being exploded from the other end.

"Can you do that?" he asked the chief petty officer.

"Count on it, sir," the old salt replied, honored to be part of whatever was underway.

Because of the nature of his plan, Will would need volunteers as daring as himself. After sending word, 275 volunteers appeared on the first day. Like his older brother Lonnie, Will commanded respect from most who served with him. Although he was known for his earlier pranks, when it

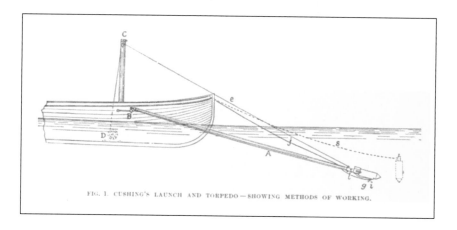

FIG. 1. CUSHING'S LAUNCH AND TORPEDO—SHOWING METHODS OF WORKING.

Schematics of final version of the torpedo designed for the attack

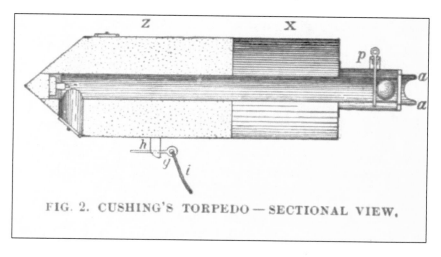

FIG. 2. CUSHING'S TORPEDO — SECTIONAL VIEW.

came to military matters, Will was a strict disciplinarian, but sailors revered him. Some even offered to forfeit any bounty for the chance to take part in one of his famed exploits. This meant that finding the 26 sailors he needed turned out to prove the easiest part of the whole plan.

His first requirement was to eliminate any married men from the list. The danger inherent in this mission seemed to offer little else than certain death. He let it be known that those wishing to sign on that they would not know what they would do until they were on their way. His only promise to them was "death, glory, or promotion."

He would take 14 with him in the lead picket boat, his choice because, even when fully loaded with men, equipment, ammunition, and weapons, they would only draw four feet of water. The other dozen men would follow in another to lend a hand if needed.

The next step circled back to Will's first thought: how to sneak up on the enemy as silently as possible. Taking blankets and makeshift insulation, he instructed the crews how to wrap the steam engines to muffle noise, having them practice so that they could get it done quickly once they were approaching the target. As the men drilled to perfect that task, the chief called him over to show the proposed design.

"Here it is, sir," he held an 18-foot iron pole in both hands, clearly proud of his design. Pointing to one end, he continued. "We'll mount an explosive canister at this end with a mechanical blasting cap and then here, at the other end, we'll mount a trigger mechanism for you to detonate the whole thing."

"Thanks, chief," Will clapped him on the shoulder. "With luck and your ingenuity, we'll take this monster down."

While the crews prepared the small ships, he took time to visit his mother. He assumed he was not going to be returning from this mission. Because his assignment was so important, he took her on a carriage ride to tell her, swearing her to secrecy.

"Mother," he said. "I have undertaken a great project, and no soul must know of it until it is accomplished, but I must tell you for I need your prayers."

She needed no more information. Her response? "I know you will do your duty."

Will returned to the shipyard, and he and his crew departed New York as October neared its end. He hoped to take advantage of the natural cover provided by a waning moon. The two vessels made their way to the Roanoke, entering the mouth of the river on the evening of the 27th.

The night was rainy and cold but, a few hours after midnight, proved fortuitous as a translucent veil of rain combined with a foggy mist hugging the water's surface to impair the vision of any lookouts. The attack team approached its target at about three in the morning.

Standing on the foredeck of the lead craft, Will spotted the outline of the CSS Albermarle at its moorings. He could smell the thick smell of burning tar from sentry bonfires and knew it would not be long before the Confederates—.

"Who goes there?" challenged one of the sentries.

"We'll soon let you know!" Will shouted back. The other Union sailors joined in the fun, shouting derisive comments and jokes. The Confederates on watch hesitated a bit watching this small and apparently lightly-armed boat coming toward them.

Will cast caution overboard and turned to his helmsman to shout, "Ahead fast!"

"Damn Yankees're out of their minds," a soldier on shore yelled to his comrades as he prepared his musket to shoot at the charging cutter.

Standing high on the prow of the lead boat, Will swung the spar-and-torpedo fixture into position. Bullets whistled past the sailors as a Rebel volley began. At the last moment, he noticed that a log boom circled his target—a floating defensive barrier that fires from shore had revealed.

"Double back," he ordered his helmsman, who turned the launch around. Will thought if they could build up enough steam, they should be able to vault the slippery obstacle. On the return approach, having gained momentum, Will's craft slid over the slime-covered barrier.

With bullets going past and around him from both the docks and the ship, Will, completely calm under fire, began working the improvised mechanism of his torpedo. He could hear the CSS Albermarle's deck-mounted cannons being fixed and turned toward him and his crew, looking up for a second to stare directly down the barrel of one of them.

Fumbling with the torpedo's release line, Will battled darkness, wet, and enemy fire to focus on the task at hand. He ignored the clang of metal on metal as the Rebel crew slammed the cascable and sealed the ammunition in the loaded cannon. He heard the loud report of the fired artillery piece and could smell the sulphureous gunpowder. However, because the launch rode low in the water, the canister flew over the crew's heads, hissing as it went by. Almost simultaneously, Will pulled on the triggering line with his right hand, detonating the torpedo beneath the CSS Albermarle with a muffled thud. The explosion tore a gaping hole in the ship's bottom and sent a tall column of water around its hull and into the air.

Will's plan seemed to have worked, but his own boat was severely damaged as well. He yelled a final command.

"Every man save himself!" Will and the others dove into cold water while being pelted with grapeshot from rifles and muskets. Once in the river, Will swam until exhausted, crawling ashore. He could hear several Confederate search parties pass close by but was only discovered by a slave who's been ordered to seek out any Union sailors he might happen upon. Naturally, the man was not as enthusiastic in completing his task. When Will saw the black man standing over him, he asked what had happened back at the berth of the CSS Albermarle.

"She is dead gone sunk," the slave told him. "And they will hang you if they catch you."

Reinvigorated by the success of his mission drove Will forward and back to his squadron. He spent the rest of the next day trying to get back to his squadron, hugging the shoreline and wading through water made prickly by the autumn cold whenever he was not hiding in the marshes.

LIEUT. CUSHING'S TORPEDO BOAT SINKING THE ALBEMARLE ON ROANOKE RIVER, N. C.

**Sepia wash depiction of the sinking of the CSS Albermarle
as rendered by R. G. Skerritt (1899)**

When he was rescued by a pilot vessel sent out as a search party, he was worn out, haggard, and scratched by thorns, biers, and branches. As bad as he looked, there was no mistaking they had found Lieutenant William Barker Cushing.

"Perhaps," he told the men who had found him, "I was unobserved because of the mud that covered me and made me blend into the earth." On October 30, 1864, he began writing up his official action report, which opened with this statement: "I have the honor to report that the rebel ironclad CSS Albermarle is at the bottom of the Roanoke River."

His idea had worked. The torpedo punctured the CSS Albermarle, sending the feared warship deep in the muddy bottom and leaving little chance of salvage.

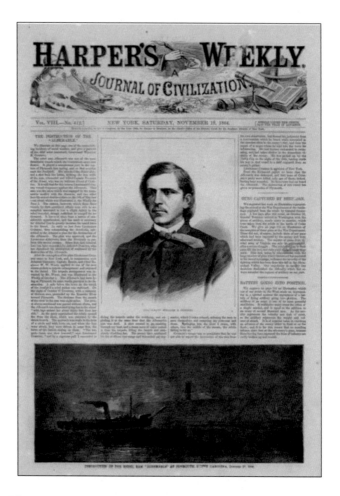

News coverage of the sinking of the CSS Albermarle

In a letter to his mother, he proudly proclaimed how "that ex-midshipman, ex-master's mate, hair-brained scapegrace" had succeeded. Once shamed at the Naval Academy, he had become the national hero of the Navy.

President Abraham Lincoln called for a proclamation of thanks from Congress, even meeting him in person. Navy Secretary Gideon Welles observed that "young Cushing was the hero of the War." One American writer who understood sea captains dedicated to the completion of their mission, Herman Melville, noted the event by writing the poem "At the Cannon's Mouth."

At the Cannon's Mouth
Herman Melville – October 1864

Palely intent, he urged his keel
Full on the guns, and touched the spring;
Himself involved in the bolt he drove
Timed with the armed hull's shot that stove
His shallop--die or do!
Into the flood his life he threw,
Yet lives--unscathed--a breathing thing
To marvel at.

He has his fame;
But that mad dash at death, how name?

Had Earth no charm to stay the Boy
From the martyr-passion? Could he dare
Disdain the Paradise of opening joy
Which beckons the fresh heart every where?
Life has more lures than any girl
For youth and strength; puts forth a share
Of beauty, hinting of yet rarer store;
And ever with unfathomable eyes,
Which baffingly entice,
Still strangely does Adonis draw.
And life once over, who shall tell the rest?
Life is, of all we know, God's best.
What imps these eagles then, that they
Fling disrespect on life by that proud way
In which they soar above our lower clay.

Pretense of wonderment and doubt unblest:
In Cushing's eager deed was shown
A spirit which brave poets own—
That scorn of life which earns life's crown;
Earns, but not always wins; but he—
The star ascended in his nativity.

After the war ended, Will continued moving up the ranks. In 1867, he was attached to the Pacific Squadron as executive officer of the USS Lancaster, the flagship of the Pacific Fleet. It was part of a flotilla making ports of call throughout Africa and Asia. While stationed in China, he proved his wild streak had not mellowed when he and a fellow crew member broke into the Forbidden City at a time when it was— quite literally—forbidden. Yet, even that breach of international protocol turned out well for him. When Imperial guards caught the two Americans, they were more concerned about being punished for dereliction of duty than they were of the foreign trespassers. The Chinese soldiers shooed them away.

Upon his return to the states in 1873, Will was transferred back to the East Coast for a patrol of Central American and the Caribbean under the auspices of the Monroe Doctrine. Nearly a decade after his best-known heroics of the Civil War, he was named commanding officer of the USS Wyoming, a sloop of war. While off the coast of Panama, Will received word that the Spanish had captured the USS Virginius, an American vessel in Cuban waters.

Although he had neither authorization nor orders, Will ordered his ship into the Caribbean to intercede. He understood that it was easier to seek forgiveness than permission.

Commander Cushing, likely on the USS Wyoming

At the time, the military governor of the island was General Juan Burriel, a man of such brutality he was nicknamed the Butcher. Living up to this nickname, Burriel began executing the crew of the Virginius as pirates.

When Will arrived and demanded an audience, Burriel refused, underestimating what he saw as a brash young American. Will had been promoted to full commander at 28—again, the youngest Naval officer ever given that rank, so he was not about to be brushed aside. His reply, devoid of any diplomacy, was a dispatch sent ashore to the general and governor. "If any more prisoners are executed," it read, "I shall open fire on the Governor's palace."

Reading the message, Burriel looked out in the harbor to see the USS Wyoming being brought broadside and setting battle stations, its crew fixing six heavy cannon barrels in his direction. Burriel understood the weight of the action and succumbed to a face-to-face. Once ashore, Burriel approached Will and held out his hand.

Will responded with a cold stare, his hands clasped behind his back, letting the general know there were to be no courtesies practiced here. Burriel was dealing with a lion, one whose pride was still keen and whose claws could still damage an opponent.

Facing Burriel down on that dock at Santiago de Cuba with such obvious abruptness and incivility spoke volumes. The military governor chafed at the rude response, but the obvious decisiveness of the young captain forced his hand. In an attempt to establish control over the situation, Burriel began lecturing him on "American interference in sovereign affairs" but was interrupted by Will, now gripping his sidearm while speaking.

"Are you going to shoot any more of the crew of the Virginius? Give me an answer; I will not be insulted again."

Burriel tried to buy time.

"*Perdoname*," Burriel told Will, softening his tone. "I truly wish I could accommodate your wishes. Unfortunately," he shrugged his shoulders, "any authorization would have to come from Havana."

"In that case, sir," Will replied, "I must request that all women and children be removed from the city, for these are not my wishes. They are my demands."

As he pivoted to return to the USS Wyoming, Will's message could not have been made any clearer. He would give the command to open fire on the city and was obviously just the sort of man to carry out any threat he made.

Burriel agreed at once to halt the executions. He realized he was faced with a warrior who was not about to grant any quarter.

That confrontation marked Will's final military victory of record. He was a gladiator in need of enemies and combat, closer to his ancestors as a Celtic berserker than a naval officer. Unfortunately, his failing health finally forced him ashore.

Will's daring recklessness put him on shaky ground throughout his life, but his impact on Naval thinking proved that effective was better than epic. Naval battles to that point had been grand and expansive; Will preferred working in a narrowly focused and personal manner. His influence on Naval warfare was so great that five naval vessels have been named in his honor, all of them some form of a fast attack ship. While he continued to serve, in December 1874, Commander. William Barker Cushing died in the presence of his wife in Washington, D.C.

He was 32 years old.

Commander William B. Cushing's grave
U.S. Naval Academy, Annapolis, Maryland

About the Author

Born into a Navy family and named in honor of the Civil War Naval hero of this book, Bill Cushing lived in Virginia, New York, Pennsylvania, Missouri, Florida, Maryland, the Virgin Islands, and Puerto Rico before moving to California. As an undergrad, he was called the "blue collar" writer by classmates at the University of Central Florida because of his own years serving in the Navy and later working as an electrician on oil tankers, naval vessels, and fishing boats before he returned to college at the age of 37. He earned an MFA in writing from Goddard College in Vermont.

For over 20 years, he taught at East Los Angeles and Mt. San Antonio colleges while residing in Glendale with his wife and their son. Recently retired, Bill continues teaching part time and facilitates a writing workshop in Eagle Rock, California for 9 Bridges, a nationwide non-profit community for writers.

As a writer, Bill has been published in various literary journals, magazines, and newspapers, including *Birders World* and *The San Juan Star*. He is a regular contributor to *L. A. Cultural Daily*. His short stories have appeared in *Borfski Press, Newtown Literary Journal, Rivanna Review,* and *Sediments* and are part of his collection of short stories, *The Commies Come to Waterton.*

His poetry has appeared in numerous journals both in print and online, including *Just a Little Cage of Bone*, a Southern Arizona Press release. Two of his poetry collections have been honored: *A Former Life* (Kops-Fetherling International Book Award) and *Music Speaks* (2019 San Gabriel Valley Chapbook Competition; 2021 New York City Book Awards.)

He is currently revising a memoir that recalls his years in the Navy and on other ships afterward and has returned to his creative thesis, *Counting*

Down the Breaths, a memoir about his late wife's death to cancer, written from the point of view of the caregiver. Southern Arizona Press released *Time Well Spent,* a collection of personal non-fiction narratives.

Previous Works

POETRY

Just a Little Cage of Bone
https://www.amazon.com/dp/1960038109

. . .this just in. . .
https://www.amazon.com/this-just/dp/8182537460/

Music Speaks
https://www.amazon.com/Music-Speaks-Bill-Cushing/dp/0359827012/

A Former Life
https://www.amazon.com/Former-Life-Bill-Cushing/dp/1635349389/

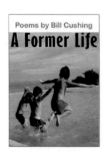

RECOLLECTION OF A LIFE

Time Well Spent
https://www.amazon.com/dp/196003846X

FICTION/SHORT STORIES

The Commies Come to Waterton
https://www.amazon.com/Commies-Come-Waterton-Bill-Cushing/dp/8119228200/

Additional Reading

Civil War Commando by Jerome Pressler

Civil War Myths and Legends by Michael R. Bradley

Commander Will Cushing by Jamie Malanowski

Commander William Barker Cushing of the United States Navy by E. M. H. Edwards

Cushing of Gettysburg by Kent Masterton Brown

Gettysburg: The Story of the Battle with Maps by M. David Detweiler and David Reisch

Lincoln's Commando by Ralph Roske and Charles Van Doren

Pickett's Charge by George R. Stewart

The Civil War: Strange & Fascinating Facts by Burke Davis

The Sea Eagle: The Civil War Memoir of Lt. Cdr. William B. Cushing USN edited by Alden R. Carter

Made in the USA
Monee, IL
14 December 2023

49206892R00033